Living in
the Moment

Living in
the Moment

Dani DiPirro

WATKINS
Sharing Wisdom Since
1893

Living in the Moment
Dani DiPirro

First published in the UK and USA in 2016
by Watkins, an imprint of Watkins
Media Limited
19 Cecil Court
London WC2N 4EZ

enquiries@watkinspublishing.co.uk

Development Editor: Kelly Thompson
Senior Editor: Fiona Robertson
Editor: Dawn Bates
Design Manager: Viki Ottewill
Design: Dani DiPirro
Production: Uzma Taj

A CIP record for this book is available
from the British Library

ISBN: 978-1-78028-937-3

10 9 8 7 6 5 4 3 2 1

Typeset in Gotham
Printed in China

www.watkinspublishing.com

To all those who have encouraged me to stay present, thank you. Your mindful spirit has inspired the creation of this book.

INTRODUCTION

Living in the moment means staying present, focusing your awareness on what's happening right now. When you stay present, you are not dwelling on the past or worrying about the future. Instead, you are engaged in your life as it is, cultivating a deep level of acceptance that can lead to improved physical and mental wellbeing. Recent research in mindfulness meditation, for example, has shown just how powerful staying in the moment can be.

But immersing yourself in the now is not easy: life moves fast these days, and recent great advances in technology offer major distractions. This book has been designed to help you focus on the art of living in the moment by pairing inspiring quotes with insights and activities to help you stay in the present, even when doing so feels challenging. Reading this book will inspire you to really make the most of every moment of your life.

Living in the Moment

phrase | liv•ing in the mo•ment

1. Fully concentrating on what's happening in the present

2. Not dwelling on the past or worrying about the future

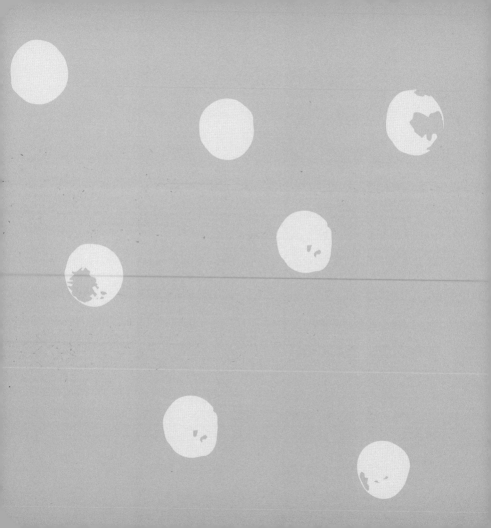

Life is **not a problem to be solved,** but a **reality to be experienced.**

Søren Kierkegaard
Danish philosopher (1813–1855)

● ● ● ● ● ● ● ● ● LIFE
● ● ● REALITY ● ● ●
EXPERIENCE ● ● ●

You may find yourself caught up with analysing your life – trying to understand how every piece of the puzzle falls into place. While you are busy problem-solving, you are missing out on the here and now. Look outward, not inward, to experience everything life has to offer.

Fully immerse yourself in your favourite activity today.

I STAY PRESENT BY DOING **WHAT I LOVE** TO DO.

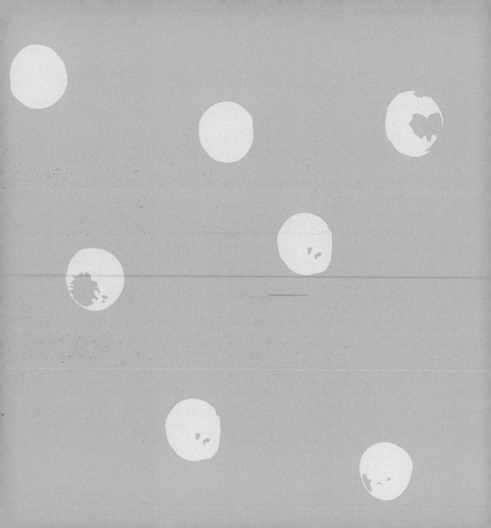

Forever is
composed
of **nows**.

Emily Dickinson
American poet (1830–1886)

FOREVER ● ● ● ● ● ● ●
● ● **COMPOSED** ● ●
● ● ● ● ● ● ● ● ● ● NOW

The future might seem like a reality, but it is not – it is a vision you have created in your mind. The only aspect of life that is completely true and real is the present moment. This is why it's essential to take each day as it comes, instead of worrying about, or trying to predict, the future.

Imagine your worries floating away from you.

I STAY PRESENT BY **NOT WORRYING** ABOUT THE FUTURE.

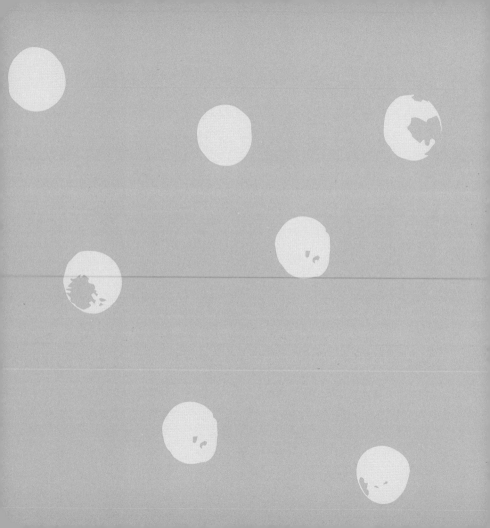

Be happy for this moment.
This moment is your life.

Omar Khayyam
Persian philosopher (1048–1131)

HAPPY

MOMENT

LIFE

In each and every day there is something worth celebrating. Take a look at your life right in this moment. What do you have today that is good and that brings you happiness? It might be your home, your family, your friends, your talents. Whatever it is, enjoy and appreciate it now.

Celebrate an accomplishment, a friendship or a joy in your life.

I STAY PRESENT
BY TRYING TO
CELEBRATE
WHAT IS.

Never let the future disturb you. You will meet it, if you have to, with the same **weapons of reason** which today arm you **against the present**.

Marcus Aurelius
Roman philosopher (AD 121-180)

TRUST

PRESENT

REASON

Fear of the future can be truly overwhelming, so try to approach challenges rationally, step by step. If you can trust in your ability to deal with anything, you will be able to relax and relish each moment. Remember, you have already survived every single bad day in your life so far!

Praise yourself for what you have already conquered.

I STAY PRESENT
BY HAVING
CONFIDENCE
IN MYSELF.

Living in the past is a **dull and lonely business;** looking back strains the neck muscles, causing you to **bump into people** not going your way.

Edna Ferber
American novelist (1885-1968)

DON'T
LOOK BACK

The past cannot be undone. If you dwell on your mistakes, you miss out on what is happening now. Imagine driving a car by only looking in the rearview mirror – you would crash within moments! Instead, free yourself from the paralysing effect of regret by focusing on the present.

Take note of three things happening in this moment.

I STAY PRESENT
BY FOCUSING
ON WHAT IS
**RIGHT IN
FRONT
OF ME.**

No **yesterdays** are ever wasted for those who **give themselves to today**.

Brendan Francis Behan
Irish poet (1923-1964)

GIVE

TODAY

FULFILLED

Truly embracing life will allow you to get the most out of each day. Life is unpredictable and not all plans work out, but you will end each day contented if you know you have given yourself fully. Then, when you finally come to the end of life, you won't look back and wonder, "What if . . . ?"

Today, do one thing your future self will thank you for.

I STAY PRESENT
BY **LIVING
TO THE
FULL.**

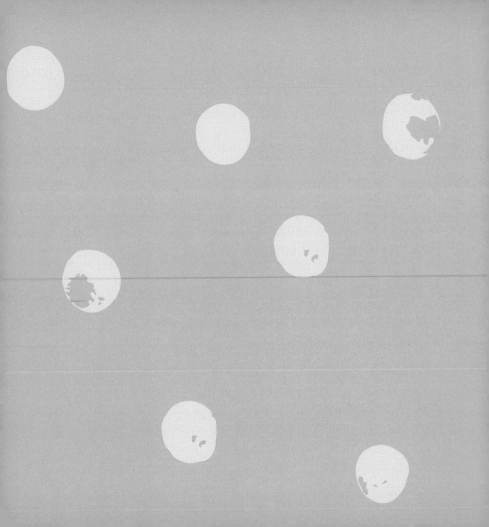

> " Everything has its wonders, **even darkness and silence**, and I learn **whatever state** I may be in, therein to be **content**.

Helen Keller
American author (1880–1968)

WONDER
CONTENTMENT
STILLNESS

Life is filled with both positive and negative experiences, and if you want to be fully present, you must embrace both the light and the dark, the good and the bad. Even the dark times are worthy of your attention and engagement because they provide inspiration, insights and perspective.

Try to observe an experience objectively.

I STAY PRESENT BY **ACCEPTING DIFFICULT TIMES.**

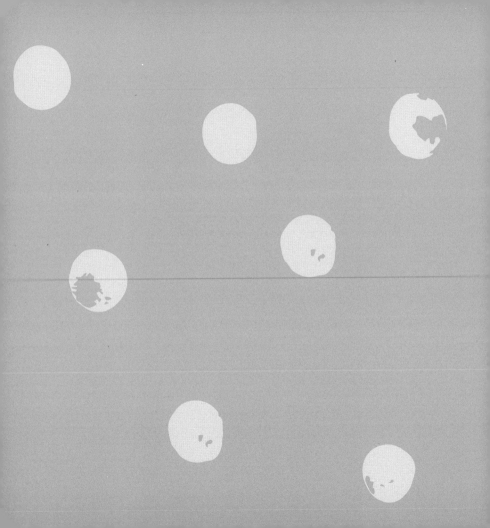

The purpose of life is to live it, **to taste experience to the utmost**, to reach out eagerly and without fear **for newer and richer experience**.

Eleanor Roosevelt
American politician (1884-1962)

PURPOSE
LIVE
FEARLESSLY

It can be tempting to stay within your comfort zone, with what is familiar and safe, as plunging into the waters of a new experience can feel scary. But in the end a comfort zone often comes to feel stale and stagnant. Only by facing up to fears and risking new challenges will you feel truly alive.

Do one thing you are scared to do.

I STAY PRESENT
BY LIVING
FEARLESSLY.

Write it on your heart
that **every day is the
best day** in the year.

Ralph Waldo Emerson
American poet (1803–1882)

HEART

TODAY

POSITIVITY

Imagine what a great day would include and then strive for that on a daily basis. Don't wait for each day to be good – make it good! Fill it with things you love, such as great music, delicious food, positive people. Set out to make every single day the best day of the year!

Treat yourself to your favourite little delight.

I STAY PRESENT
BY MAKING
TODAY A
GOOD DAY.

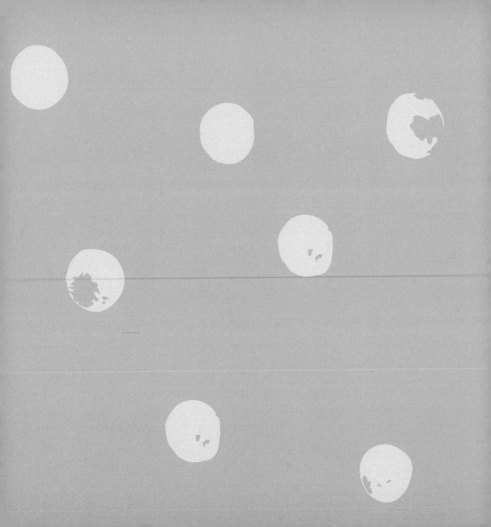

" Dost thou **love life?**
Then **do not squander
time**, for that's the
stuff life is made of.

Benjamin Franklin
American inventor (1706-1790)

LOVE

LIFE

ACTION

It is so easy to waste time – sleeping the morning away, watching mindless TV, fearing the future or regretting the past. Keep reminding yourself that each day has only 24 hours and you need to make them count! To get the most out of life, pay attention to what you do with your time.

Evaluate how you spend your time on a daily basis.

I STAY PRESENT BY **USING MY TIME WELL.**

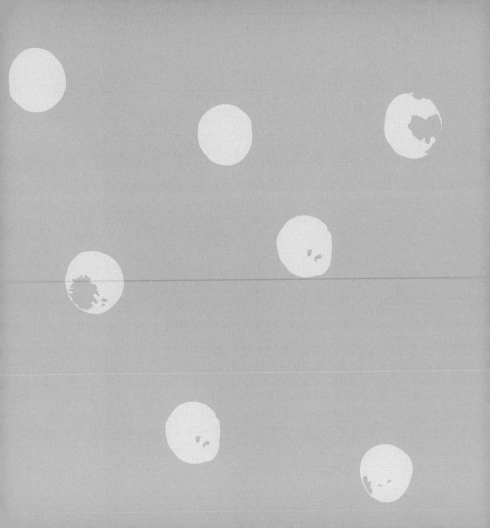

All conditioned things are **impermanent**. When one sees this with **wisdom**, one turns away from suffering.

Gautama Buddha
Founder of Buddhism (563–483 BC)

EPHEMERAL APPRECIATION WISDOM

Nothing lasts for ever. But rather than think of this in a negative way, try reframing the thought so you see it as encouragement to embrace every moment with enthusiasm. Doing so will turn difficulties into opportunities to learn and grow.

Indulge in a once-in-a-lifetime opportunity today.

I STAY PRESENT
BY SEEING ALL
MOMENTS AS
UNIQUE.

Change your life today.
Don't gamble on the
future, **act now**,
without delay.

Simone de Beauvoir
French writer (1908–1986)

NOW

ACTION

CHANGE

It is all too easy to postpone things until tomorrow, but the present moment is the only one you are guaranteed. Every moment is an opportunity for action or change. So make a call you have been putting off, apply for a new job – whatever it is you need to do, take your first step right now!

Cross off at least one thing on your to-do list today.

I STAY PRESENT BY **TAKING ACTION NOW.**

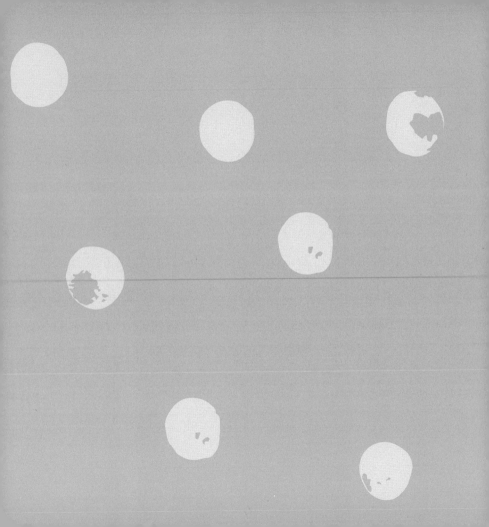

Chance is always powerful. Let your hook be always cast; in the pool where you **least expect it**, there will be a fish.

Ovid
Roman poet (43 BC–AD 17)

READINESS

POWERFUL

CHANCE

You never know what great opportunities might come your way. It is important to be ready to take advantage of them and be open to change. Be receptive not only to the chances that present themselves to you, but also to ways you can create your own luck from events that unfold.

Keep your eyes (and heart) open to opportunities.

I STAY PRESENT BY EMBRACING CHANCE.

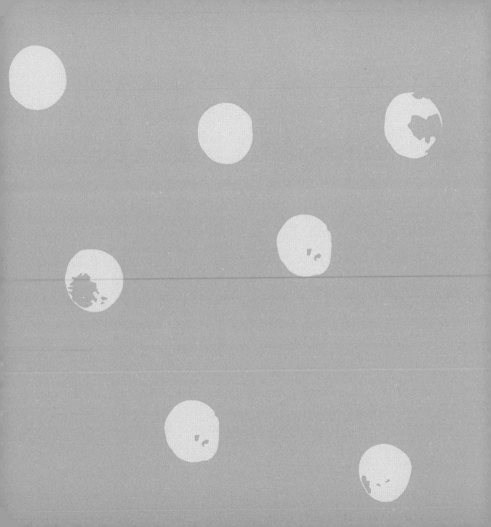

The **price** of anything is the amount of **life** you **exchange** for it.

Henry David Thoreau
American author (1817–1862)

VALUE

TIME

AWARE

It can be enlightening to count up how much time you spend on activities you enjoy, and how much on those you do not. Life is measured in a series of such moments. We can't always do exactly what we want, of course, but it's important to think about what matters most to you.

Say no to activities that don't add value to your life.

I STAY PRESENT
BY LEARNING
TO **SAY NO**.

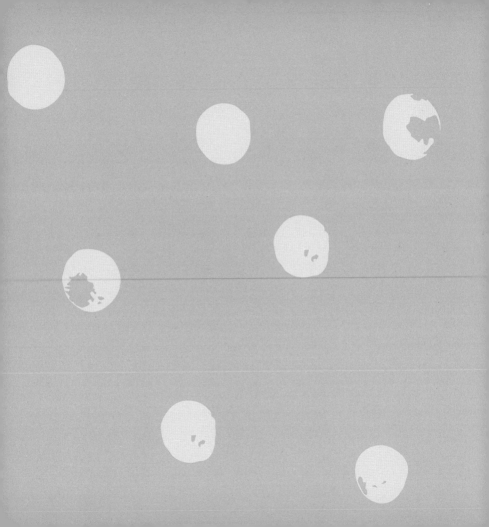

I am an old man and have known **a great many troubles**, but most of them **never happened**.

Mark Twain
American author (1835-1910)

ENJOY

PRESENCE

PEACE

Think about the last time you fretted over something to come. Did it turn out as badly as you thought? Most things we worry about never actually happen, which means we have wasted precious time thinking about them – time we could have spent enjoying the present moment.

Write down your worries, and then set them aside.

I STAY PRESENT BY **LETTING GO** OF MY WORRIES.

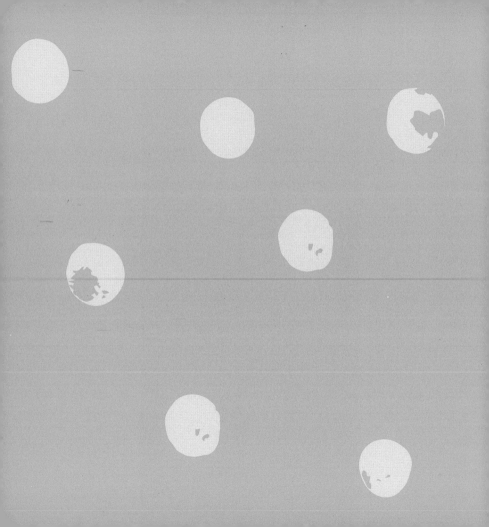

" In order for the **light** to
shine so brightly, the
darkness must be **present**.

Francis Bacon
English philosopher (1561-1626)

LIGHT

BALANCE

DARKNESS

The balance between life's light and dark is what makes being alive wonderful. Without the difficult moments, you would be unable to fully embrace the good times. Try to accept the stormy stretches of your journey, with an awareness that you are doing the best you can and they will soon pass.

Can you be thankful for something bad that happened to you?

I STAY PRESENT
BY **ACCEPTING**
BOTH THE
LIGHT
AND THE
DARK.

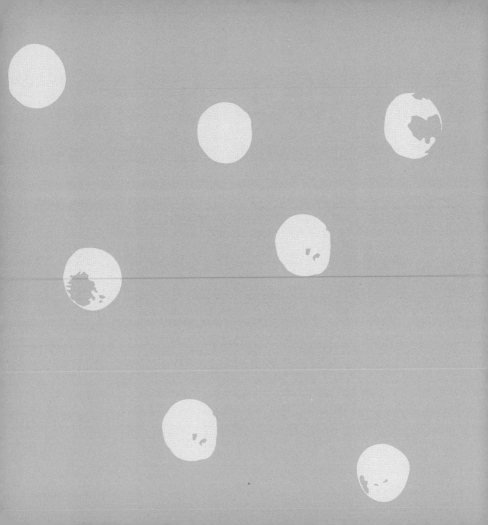

The **only journey** is the journey **within**.

Rainer Maria Rilke
Austrian poet (1875–1926)

EMBRACE

INNER

JOURNEY

Being mindful means being aware of what's happening within you as well as around you. Noticing your personal journey is a vital part of living in the moment, so try paying close attention to what you are thinking and feeling at certain times. Why does a person or situation make you feel that way?

Listen closely to your thoughts and feelings as you go about your day.

I STAY PRESENT
BY BEING
**AWARE
OF HOW
I FEEL.**

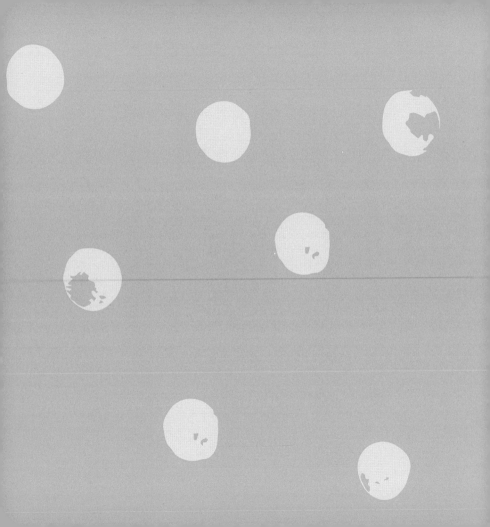

Sit in reverie and watch the changing colour of the waves that break upon the idle **seashore of the mind.**

Henry Wadsworth Longfellow
American poet (1807–1882)

MINDFUL
MOMENT   OBSERVE

One of the best ways you can practise living in the moment is by sitting quietly and observing the world around you and within you. Instead of striving to cross off a task or move on to the next thing, calmly engage with this moment, here and now, and be fully aware of each shift that takes place.

Sit still for as long as you can today.

I STAY PRESENT
BY OBSERVING
EVERY
SINGLE
MOMENT.

TOP 10 WAYS TO LIVE IN THE MOMENT

1. Focus on your five senses.

2. Avoid multi-tasking.

3. Do all things with patience.

4. Enjoy time spent alone.

5. Practise deep breathing.

6. Avoid dwelling on your past.

7. Observe your thoughts objectively.

8. Do what you love to do.

9. Sit quietly and try to still your mind.

10. Go for a walk and soak up nature.

TOP 10  WAYS TO STAY PRESENT AT WORK

1. Do only one task at a time.

2. Be aware of how long each task takes.

3. Declutter your work space.

4. Pay attention to how you are sitting.

5. Take breaks from your desk.

6. Put your phone away in meetings.

7. Schedule email-free time.

8. Be aware of the tools you use.

9. Try standing at your desk for calls.

10. Really listen to your co-workers.

TOP 10 WAYS TO STAY PRESENT AT HOME

1. Have screen-free time.

2. Sit down for meals and eat mindfully.

3. Give loved ones your full attention.

4. Appreciate each unique room.

5. Light a scented candle and relish it.

6. Wear your favourite outfit.

7. Take a long bath or shower.

8. Do something soothing.

9. Get rid of what you don't need.

10. List the best things about your home.

**TOP 10** **WAYS TO STAY PRESENT WITH OTHERS**

1. Be open about your feelings.

2. Listen without thinking about what to say.

3. Don't look at a screen while talking.

4. Give long, thoughtful hugs.

5. Notice what you love about others.

6. Use a person's name in conversation.

7. Share your goals and dreams.

8. Speak with a calm, loving tone.

9. Make consistent eye contact.

10. Do something you both love.

TOP 10 WAYS TO STAY PRESENT IN LOVE

1. Enjoy treating your loved one.

2. Focus on their best qualities.

3. Spend lots of time together.

4. Try a new activity together.

5. Give lots of heartfelt compliments.

6. Listen closely and carefully.

7. Remember to smile at each other.

8. Do something silly together.

9. Share how you feel often.

10. Always act with kindness.

NOTE TO READER

Hello! I'm Dani. I hope you've enjoyed reading this little book as much as I enjoyed creating it. Living in the moment is such an important part of my life, and I truly believe everyone can benefit from striving to stay more present.

In 2009 I created **PositivelyPresent.com**. Since setting up that website, I've gone on to write multiple ebooks and publish *The Positively Present Guide to Life*, as well as designing diaries for Watkins' *Every Day Matters* series.

I also work as a graphic designer. Balancing so many different aspects of life can be challenging, but striving for mindfulness helps me manage it all. Doing my best to live in the moment has transformed my life – and I hope it will do the same for yours!

If you want to learn more about me or my work, check out **DaniDiPirro.com**, or visit **PositivelyPresent.com** for inspiration on living positively in the present.